Some people have two Dads

For Steven and Riccardo - L.P.
For Lily and Atticus - F.K.

If you can, please buy two books - one for your child
and one to give away as a present or donation to a school
or library so together we can educate parents, children
and the community and make the world a better place.

www.Somefamilies.net

First published 2012

Text copyright © Luca Panzini and Fabri Kramer 2012
Illustrations copyright © Luca Panzini 2012
All rights reserved

ISBN: 1478383659   ISBN-13: 978-1478383659

Some people have two Dads

By Luca Panzini and Fabri Kramer

Illustrated by Luca Panzini

"Good morning angel" Daddy whispers as he gently strokes Daisy's hair.

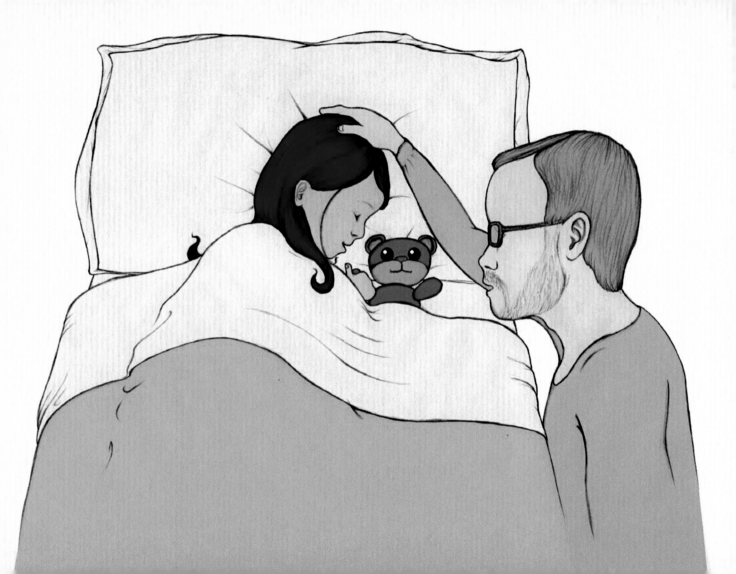

Daisy opens her eyes, jumps out of bed and screams, "Yaaaaaay! It is my Birthday!"

Daisy is very excited and cannot wait to get ready for her party.

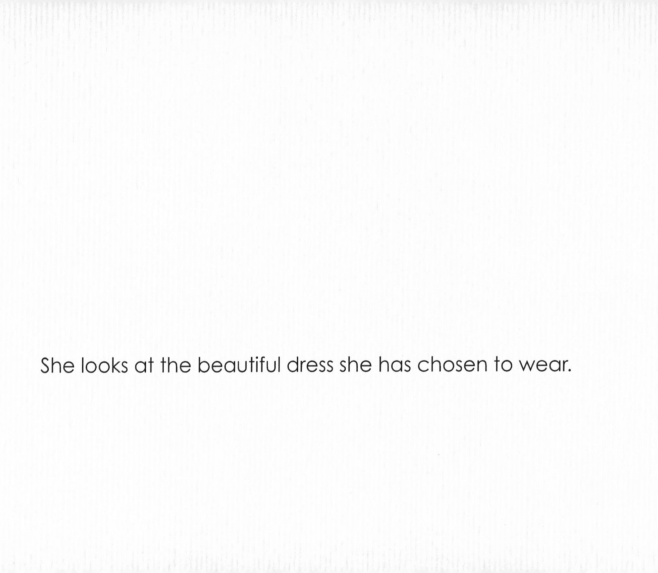

She looks at the beautiful dress she has chosen to wear.

Once she is ready,
Papi wishes Daisy a happy birthday
and gives her a very large present.

Daisy opens it very carefully.

Inside is a beautiful portrait of her family that Papi has painted for her. Daisy is thrilled and squeezes Papi with thanks.

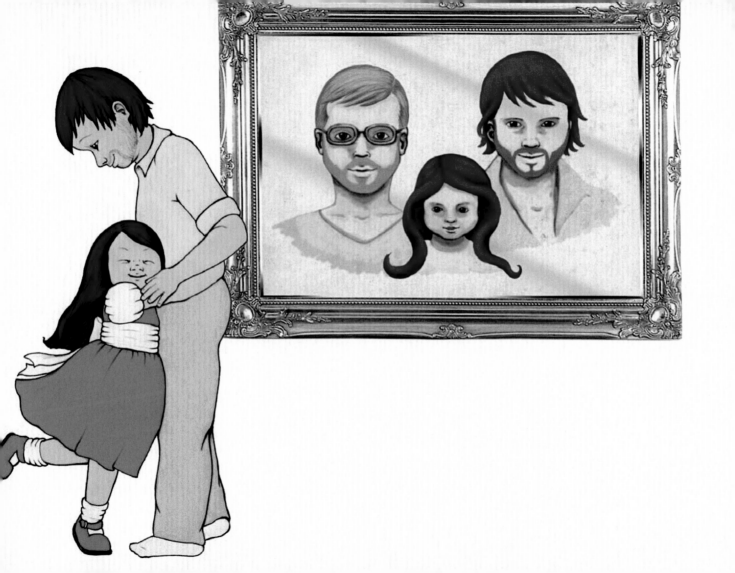

Like every year on her birthday
Daisy smiles at her Daddies and asks
"tell me again about when I was born."

"Well," Papi says, "the story begins when I met your Daddy."

"We loved each other very much and after a while decided that we wanted a family of our own."

"But Daddies cannot carry babies..."
Daisy giggles as she imagines her Daddies with big bellies.

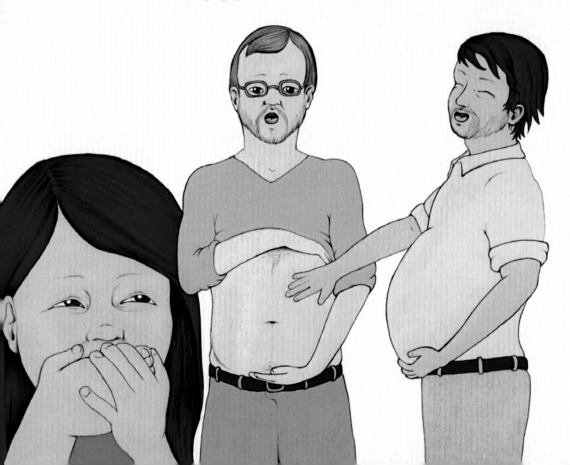

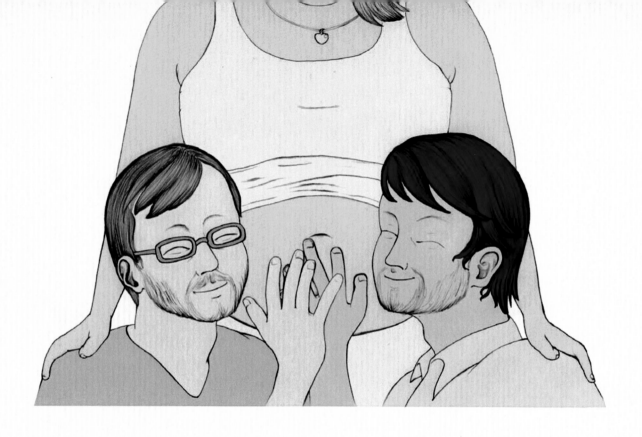

"We met a lovely lady called Meg. She saw how much love we had and offered to have our baby for us."

"The following summer you were born. You were the sweetest baby in the whole world."

Daddy and I could not stop smiling because we were so happy to have our beautiful little girl."

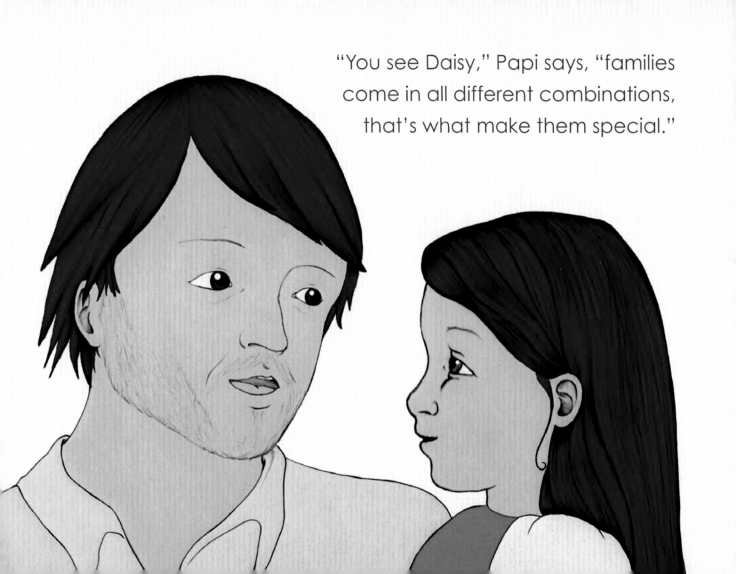

"You see Daisy," Papi says, "families come in all different combinations, that's what make them special."

Some people have one mum...

...some people have one dad,

...some people have two mums,

some people have one mum and one dad,

some people have one dad and two mums."

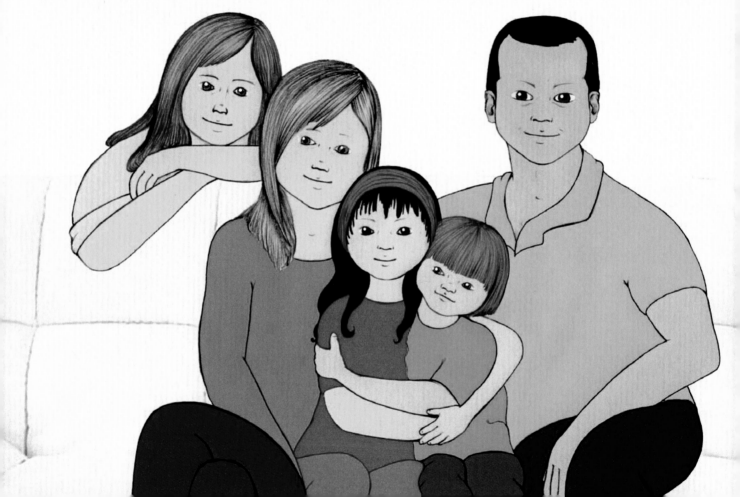

Daisy smiles as her Daddies both kiss her and says,
"and I am so lucky to have my two daddies."

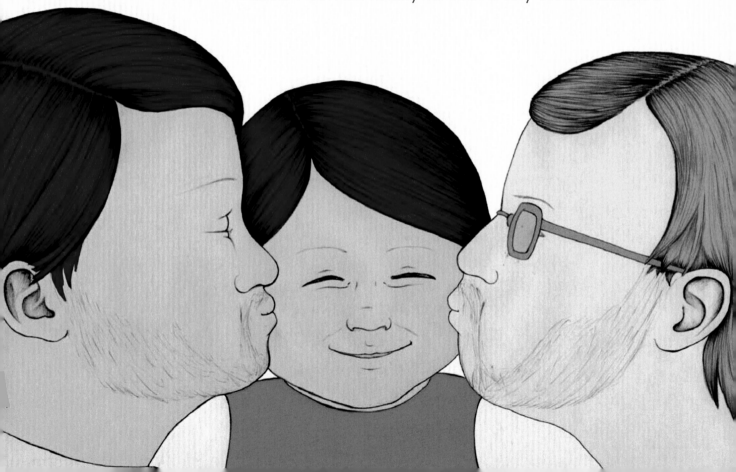

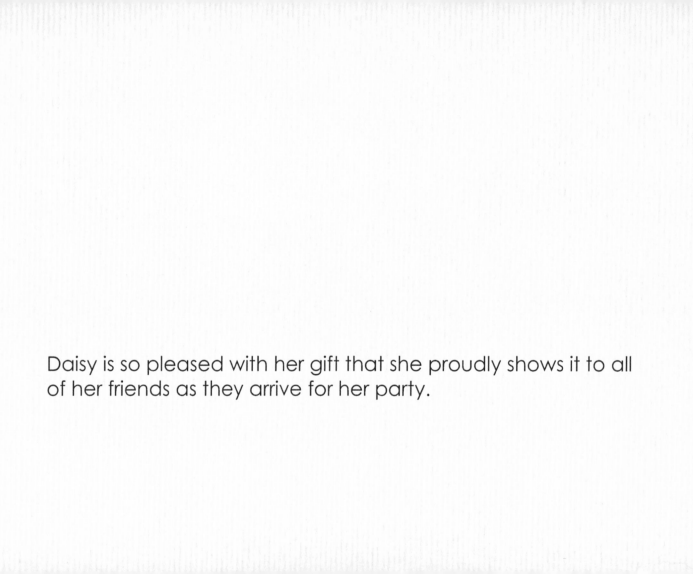

Daisy is so pleased with her gift that she proudly shows it to all of her friends as they arrive for her party.

As she blows out the candles on her birthday cake, Daisy's wish is that she will remember this special day forever.

At the end of such an exciting day Daisy falls asleep, a very happy and much loved little girl.

The end.

Made in the USA
San Bernardino, CA
18 January 2015